The Productive Academic Writer

An Easy-To-Read Guide to Low-Stress Prolific Writing

Kasthurirangan Gopalakrishnan, Ph.D.

Transdependenz LLC

Editorial Reviews for "The Productive Academic Writer"

"An interesting introductory guide to writing, which is very useful for both academics and non-academics."

Dr. Miklas Scholz
Professor & Chair in Civil Engineering,
University of Salford, Greater Manchester, UK

"If you have had the intention to write something, but you have not been able to achieve your goal, *The Productive Academic Writer* will explain why you haven´t and what you can do to make your intentions a reality... *The Productive Academic Writer* is a motivation road towards writing. It offers the reader the possibility to detect their blocks as well as the different ways to overcome them. I am sure academic writing teachers and writers, in general, really appreciate being understood by another writer, Gopalakrishnan, who had the time to present our doubts and common stressful situations with answers to overcome all of them."

Dr. Beatriz Manrique
Professor, Department of Modern Languages,
University of Zulia, Maracaibo, Venezuela

"I will definitely recommend this book to my students and colleagues. It has also helped me a lot to recognize problems that I have with writing. For me, the added value is the concise, yet extremely valuable, exposition of the problems that potential writers face leading to failure in writing, and how to overcome them. Easy-to-read, convince yourself and you're writing."

Dr. Rogelio Palomera-Garcia
Professor, Department of Electrical & Computer Engineering, University of Puerto Rico at Mayaguez, Puerto Rico

"The book provides easily digestible advises on academic writing. It is written in simple language and has many practical examples and advises."

Dr. Martins Zaumanis
Project Manager, Latvian State Roads Department, Riga, Latvia

"There are plenty books on the market telling the would-be author (academic or otherwise) how to write with clarity and grammatical precision. There are fewer books dealing with the issue of how to get motivated to write in the first place. That's why "The Productive Academic Writer" is so useful, for it provides sound advice, which, if followed, is sure to make the would-be writer more disciplined and productive…Although this book is primarily written for people in academia (where one's job often depends on written productivity), anyone who writes a lot, whether as an avocation or a career, will benefit from its advice."

Dr. Doug Erlandson (Amazon Top 50 Reviewer)
Adjunct Instructor of Philosophy, Southeast Community College, Lincoln, NE, USA

"The Productive Academic Writer, like the subtitle suggests, is an easy to read primer that applies simple time management skills to writing in an academic context. The book gives lots of tips and ideas for getting started immediately. Would recommend to anyone getting started on academic writing, but unsure where to start."

Sugu Althomsons
English Instructor, Kansai International Academy, Osaka, Japan

"The Productive Academic Writer is a timely help for me, a novice researcher who always struggles with the task academic writing and feels stressed out by it…For academics aspiring to improve their writing productivity, it is an "engaging and easy-to-read" book worth reading and remembering."

Dr. Weiqiang Wang
School of English for International Business, Guangdong University of Foreign Studies, China

"Kasturirangan Gopalakrishanan's "The Productive Academic Writer" is an edifying, enlivening and enlightening book. Written in a reader-friendly style, its tenor and tone are ideally suited to address and accomplish its principal objective: arming its academic readership with the much needed courage, confidence and clarity to navigate the epistemic terrain, which is often fraught with untold anguishes and angst... Any discerning academic reader of the book will applaud its novelty and vibrancy and so will be delighted to add it to their "keepsake" collection. Switch on and read on then the Productive Academic Writer to become a prolific academic writer!"

Dr. S. Sivasubramaniam
Assoc. Professor, Department of Language Education, University of the Western Cape, South Africa

CONTENTS

Dedicated to my

Teachers

With utmost gratitude!

⌘

"Beware what you set your heart upon,
for it surely shall be yours"

- Ralph Waldo Emerson

⌘

PREFACE

The Guardian, a British national daily newspaper, recently featured a news article on how the intense pressure of graduate, post-doctoral study, and early-career academia can be quite stressful leading to mental health problems. The "demand for increased product and productivity" was blamed as the primary cause for "rising levels of mental health problems among academics". If you like, you can read the full article here: http://goo.gl/C1DuH7.

Graduate students need to produce journal articles and conference papers to graduate. While the internet age has opened up access to all kinds of information available never before, the burden now rests on the students to stay up-to-date with the state-of-the-art research advancements at the global level. The consequence is that most students are forced to subscribe to the culture of rapid scanning and skimming of pieces of information from multiple electronic sources with very little time to concentrate and contemplate on the actual research questions. As someone rightly said, "these days we click a lot of links, read less, and remember even lesser".

The writing productivity of graduate students is under siege from multiple directions: finding the fine balance between their coursework and research, managing time wisely amidst all the distractions, the pressure to find a job after graduation, etc.

Postdocs and researchers are under similar pressure to publish and write proposals to secure funding on an ongoing basis.

Young tenure-track faculty are working harder and harder to meet the promotion and tenure requirements which are becoming stricter year by year. First, scholarship in most disciplines was measured in terms of number of publications which created the publish-or-perish syndrome. With the increasing number of open-access journals all over the place, the emphasis then shifted to the number of publications one needs to have in high-impact Science Citation Indexed (SCI) journals. Now, the number of citations and H-index have taken the high seat.

Each discipline and university will have its own requirements for promotion and tenure, but everyone would agree that the pressure on young faculty to publish is enormous in the middle of often overloaded teaching and service responsibilities.

Without going through all the details, it is suffice to mention that our personal and social lives add their own flavor to our already stressed-out lives.

My aim in going through this is not to enlist the number of excuses to justify why academicians can't write, but to underscore the need for some compassion towards ourselves and empathy towards our colleagues in similar situations. We deserve every bit of encouragement first from ourselves to keep going. In other words, let us not be too hard on ourselves!

By saying this, I am in no way encouraging some sort of self-indulgence or complacency. But, productive academic writers are those who realistically strive for excellence in their pursuit of writing goals with a down-to-earth attitude.

Bullying, calling names, punishment, and pressure tactics are negative, fear-inducing strategies that can never truly inspire anyone. Rather, they lead to more severe problems than the ones they originally intended to solve. On the other hand, genuine appreciation and positive reinforcement of even the minor efforts made towards our goals has far-reaching positive implications leading to high levels of low-stress productivity. This will be a recurring theme of this book.

There are already so many good books on this subject, so what was the need for one more book like this, you ask. A valid question. In one sense, there is nothing new in this book that has not been discussed before. The aim was not to create new knowledge or new strategies to productive writing as such, but present available information on this topic in an easy-to-read, and hopefully engaging manner.

I have tried to present proven productivity strategies and tips in a way that doesn't demand you to add more activities to your already stressed-out schedule. Rather, this book's aim is to assist you to do what you are already doing more effectively and efficiently with minimal stress, and possibly to identify and eliminate those activities and habits that interfere with your writing productivity. In other words, be productive and have a happy life!

Considering the vast body of existing information on this topic, this book has heavily drawn on the work of others. The author cannot fail to acknowledge with deep gratitude the contributions made by every individual whose work is referenced in this book.

⌘

"Never discourage anyone …who continually makes progress, no matter how slow."

- Plato

⌘

CHAPTER 1
INTRODUCTION

"Everywhere I go I'm asked if I think the university stifles writers. My opinion is that they don't stifle enough of them."

– *Flannery O'Connor*

❧

Academic writing is hard. You may wonder why I begin this book on an apparently negative note. Well, I could have started it by saying "academic writing is the easiest and most lovable task that you can ever imagine". May be for some. But, for most of us students, post-docs, researchers, and professors, that's far from the truth. Most of the time, we just have the opposite experience - at least when it comes to getting the writing done.

We don't seem to mind reading other's work, doing the research, collecting the data, conducting data analysis, interpreting the data, etc. And, we definitely enjoy the moment and even celebrate when our work is published with our name on it in the form of a journal article or a book chapter or a book. But, we do seem to resist what comes in between these two – the writing process.

no
inspiration

Have you had the excruciating experience of sitting in front of the computer and staring at the monitor hoping that words would start appearing magically forming sentences and paragraphs? Have you ever given up after starting a manuscript resigning to the idea that you just don't have enough time to complete it now, but that you will come back to it later which never happened? How many times have you determined that you'll use those summer months to finish writing up your pending papers and proposals, but never followed through?

Instead of a simple 'yes' or 'no' answer to these questions, it will be very helpful to take a minute or two to examine the reasons behind those answers.

How do we become a productive academic writer?

Before going any further, let us try to understand what we mean by the term "productive" here. Productivity is about "the effective and efficient use of all resources" *within one's capacity*. Note the emphasis on one's capacity in this definition. What this means is that one person's capacity can vary from another. Our goal in this book is to vaporize the disempowering roadblocks on the path to productive writing in order to avail our full writing potential.

So, what is your biggest writing challenge? What holds you from productive writing? Is it just one thing you have identified or it a vague list that you have not yet been able to put your finger on? Researchers and practitioners in the field of psychology and education have worked hard over the years to get us some answers.

Psychology is the study of why we do what we do, to state it simply. Psychologists study individual and social behavior and their relation to mental functions.

Robert Boice, now an Emeritus Professor of Psychology at Stony Brook University is known worldwide for his research and publications on faculty development and progress. Much of his work has focused on helping young faculty balance their research and classroom instruction and improve their writing productivity so that they can more effectively serve as educators.

Based on Boice's extensive research, the following could be considered as some major categories of hindrances to productive academic writing:

- **Perfectionism** (Blatt 1995): "...involves exceedingly high, self-imposed, unrealistic standards and an intensive self-scrutiny and criticism in which there is an inability accept flaws, faults, or failure within oneself across multiple domains. In short, it consists of an active striving to be flawless." Since, this could be a major hindrance, the first two chapters of this book are devoted to this topic.

- **Procrastination**: postponing that which is necessary to reach some goal by allowing low-priority tasks get in the way of high-priority tasks. Procrastination is a disempowering habit that could have multiple causes, including perfectionism, limiting beliefs ("I cannot write unless I feel inspired", "I need large blocks of undisrupted time to write", etc.) as well as real external challenges like illness, childcare, elder-care, family issues, etc. Boice (1989) links procrastination of scholarly writing to "patterns of bingeing one's work and of complaining about busyness".

- **Lack of accountability**: Boice (1989) refers to universities as "loosely coupled systems" or "organized anarchies" where there is no built-accountability for ensuring timely writing and publishing. This is especially true for young professors who typically end up spending more time preparing for teaching and over-committing to other activities besides writing.

- **Other hindrances**: this can include emotional blocks (fear of failure or success, a feeling of creativity vacuum where one feels an inability to generate and incubate ideas, going through stressful situations in one's personal life like divorce, pregnancy, etc.), unfriendly workplace (bullying boss, departmental politics, negative rumors, noisy neighbors, etc.), chronic health issues, financial problems, repeated rejections, distractions, etc. which can all be arising from perfectly legitimate concerns.

After experimenting with different solutions to academic writing productivity issues, Boice (1992) demonstrated the effectiveness of combining four proven strategies (free writing, writing on a schedule, confidence-building mindset, and making writing a social activity) to overcome writing blocks rather than relying on a single strategy. His four-step plan forms the foundation of most books on productive academic writing published to date, including this book.

Freewriting or unedited stream-of-consciousness writing (where you just write what comes to your mind without any editing or stopping, no matter what) is a key strategy to break free from the heavy inertia and gain momentum in writing the 'messy' first draft. It is a positive habit-building technique as well as the fastest and easiest way to get your unstructured thoughts to flow through your fingertips onto the paper or the monitor. More to come on this in a later chapter.

According to Boice (1992), productive academic writers (he refers to them as quick starters in his study) have the following commonalities that serve as ideal traits to be emulated by aspiring prolific writers:

- They show a unique willingness to jump into writing instead of waiting for the ideal conditions to get them started (such as availability of large time blocks, preparedness, etc.)

- They exhibit far less bingeing behavior in writing, preparation for teaching, research, etc. because they try to plan everything and 'carry out the essential activities in brief, daily sessions'. For instance, they achieve their writing goals by writing daily in small 1-3 hour stints.

- They are intentional in what they do and reinforce their healthy writing habits through positive affirmations rather than indulging in negative self-talk.

- They make their writing goals public and seek out and connect with other colleagues for advice, support and guidance on writing.

Although our writing productivity is often constrained by a number of external factors that are beyond our control, it is possible that there are some internal changes (such as giving up limiting beliefs and accepting the mindset of prolific writers) we can make that can have major positive impact on our scholarly output.

As someone who has embraced a career in academia or preparing oneself to take up one, the core of our professional success and reputation depends on scholarly writing, be it in the form of an article, proposal, journal/conference paper, book chapter, etc. We are primarily evaluated by our peers and superiors by the quality, quantity, and impact of our publications and our ability to secure funding (which in turn is linked to writing solid proposals that sell!).

While writing is hard, what we'll learn in this book is that, it is possible for anyone to develop a healthy habit of writing by making simple behavioral changes and shifts in thinking about academic writing.

For instance, if we approach writing as a pleasurable experience that adds significant value to the quality of our lives (a medium to develop and hone your thinking and communication skills, a time for quiet reflection in a fast-paced environment, etc.), then we'll not consider it a drudgery, but will more easily adopt the habit of daily writing.

We don't need to be a born-writer nor is it a skill that is only meant to be acquired by the chosen few. All it takes is consistent, disciplined and focused efforts. The more we deliberately practice it, the more we become perfect at it (Ericcson et al. 1993). This is true for any skill, including writing.

It is crucial to understand that each individual is unique and what works for me may not work for you and vice versa. There is no single writing method that works for everyone. So, please don't think of the strategies discussed in this book as something set on stone. You may find all of them to be working for you or none of them working for you. It is no big deal.

You are welcome to take cues from these strategies and customize them or even better, develop your own writing strategies, based on these principles, that better suits your needs and circumstances.

I do hope that you'll be able to discover the writing method that works best for you after reading this book.

Blatt, S. (1995). The Destructiveness of Perfectionism: Implications for the Treatment of Depression. American Psychologist, Vol. 50, No. 12, pp. 1003-1020. Available at: http://goo.gl/PbQxU7

> *Self-oriented perfectionism involves exceedingly, high self-imposed, unrealistic standards, and an intensive self-scrutiny and criticism in which there is an inability accept flaws, faults or failure within oneself across multiple domains. In short, it consists of an active striving to be flawless.*

Boice, R. (1982). Increasing the Writing Productivity of 'Blocked' Academicians. Behavior Research Therapy, Vol. 20, pp. 197-207.

Boice presents case histories of 6 academicians who sought remedy for writer's 'block'. The subjects came from a diverse group which goes to show that anyone in the academic setting can go through periods of unproductivity in writing at any stage in one's career for a variety of reasons: a well-established male professor, a male doctoral student, a male health-professional in an applied setting, a female assistant professor, a male administrator in an academic setting, and a female assistant professor who was deeply distressed at the prospect of not securing tenure because of not being able to write. Boice (1982) made some interesting observations as he set out to administer his 'contingency management' treatment package:

> *Writers who complain of unproductiveness tend to avoid actual writing and by engaging in alternative activities...Writing, although an individual activity, is seemingly facilitated by social support...Small, steady amounts of writing are preferable to large bursts of output which are impractical to sustain...Complaints of an inability to write are related to poor skills in the management of both writing situations and writing times....The subjects overcome fear of criticism and ideas of perfection once writing became a reinforcing and habitual activity.*

Boice, R. (1989). Procrastination, Busyness and Bingeing. Behavior Research Therapy, Vol. 27, No. 6, pp. 605-611.

True, professors know that writing for publication is a greater determination of survival and other career rewards than any other professional activity (Boice and Jones, 1984). But, they also know that writing is a difficult task, one demanding long-term efforts and threatening real risks of rejection and embarrassment. Thus, many new professors fall prey to the busyness of preparing for teaching.

Boice, R. (1992). Combining Writing Block Treatments: Theory and Research. Behavior Research and Therapy, Vol. 30, No. 2, pp. 107-116.

The harsh reality of facilitating writing fluency, unlike the magical solutions that may await those of us who aspire to become, say, good sketch artists (Edwards, 1979), is that it requires nothing less than hard work with an unwavering eye to efficiency and improvement.

Ericsson, K. A., Krampe, R. T., and Tesch-Romer, C. (1993). The Role of Deliberate Practice in the Acquisition of Expert Performance. Psychological Review, Vol. 100, No. 3, pp. 363-406.

We view elite performance as the product of a decade or more of maximal efforts to improve performance in a domain through an optimal distribution of deliberate practice...The commitment to deliberate practice distinguishes the expert performer from the vast majority of children and adults who seem to have remarkable difficulty meeting the much lower demands on practice in schools, adult education, and in physical exercise programs.

Mikhailova, E. A. and Nilson, L. B. (2007). Developing Prolific Scholars: The "Fast Article Writing" Methodology. Journal of Faculty Development, Vol. 22, No. 2, pp. 93-100. Available at: http://goo.gl/jyo2Wl

The fast article methodology can be best described then as a step-by-step process that facilitates and optimizes the article-writing and publication process, communication and collaboration with co-authors, and the mentoring of graduate students in thesis and article writing.

Shaw, C. and Ward, L. (2014). Dark Thoughts: Why Mental Illness is on the Rise in Academia. The

Guardian. Guardian News and Media Limited. Available at: http://goo.gl/C1DuH7.

> *Mental health problems are on the rise among UK academics amid the pressures of greater job insecurity, constant demand for results and an increasingly marketised higher education system.*

> *University counselling staff and workplace health experts have seen a steady increase in numbers seeking help for mental health problems over the past decade, with research indicating nearly half of academics show symptoms of psychological distress.*

Zerubavel, E. (2001). The Clockwork Muse: A Practice Guide to Writing Theses, Dissertations, and Books. Harvard University Press, Cambridge, MA.

> *Unfortunately, writing is an activity that tends to evoke a considerable amount of anxiety, often resulting in the paralytic condition commonly known as a "writer's block.*

⌘

"*Two roads diverged in a wood, and I—I took the one less traveled by, And that has made all the difference.*"

- Robert Frost

⌘

CHAPTER 2
OVERCOME YOUR LIMITING BELIEFS

*"Drop the idea that you are Atlas carrying
the world on your shoulders. The world
would go on even without you. Don't take
yourself so seriously."*

- *Norman Vincent Peale*

In this Chapter, we'll challenge some of the self-
limiting beliefs and myths about productive writing
and discuss some practical strategies to overcome
them.

THE PERFECTIONIST MINDSET

"It is impossible to live without failing at something, unless you live so cautiously that you might as well not have lived at all – in which case, you fail by default."

– J. K. Rowling (Commencement Address at Harvard University, 2008)

❅

It was John Justrite's first attempt at writing a journal article. He wanted it to be the 'perfect' paper although he didn't know quite what it meant. As he sat in front of his laptop, with his hands poised over the keyboard, thoughts of his article appearing on the front cover of Nature magazine ran through his mind. He immediately pointed his internet browser to the Nature magazine website and started going through the articles from the latest issue.

After aimlessly spending about an hour skimming through the articles and contemplating how he'll soon publish at least two articles in every issue of Nature, it suddenly dawned upon him that he had to send out the draft abstract of his paper and the outline to his adviser in an hour or so.

John felt that his opening sentence in the abstract should be a killer. He reasoned that it should be so perfect to be able to convey the whole paper in that one sentence and yet be so crisp such that it captures the minds of his reviewers and readers.

He immediately typed "The" and paused waiting for the next perfect word. "Should it be 'purpose' or 'objective'?" he zeroed in on those two words after thinking of various possibilities for 30 minutes. But, he felt that most papers started that way and that's why they end up being of mediocre quality.

He looked up for synonyms in the thesaurus, but was not satisfied with what he found. He then typed "how do perfect papers begin" in Google to explore other options…

John Justrite may be experiencing an exaggerated version of the perfectionist syndrome, but often times our writing productivity is marred by even a milder version of the perfectionist mindset, especially when we are faced with what we perceive to be a mammoth writing project.

It is true that we don't want our final product to be of a low-grade quality fit to be trashed after spending all that time and effort. But, we fail to realize that our first draft is not the final draft.

The biggest challenge to our productivity is to get that first draft out. Once we have the first draft in whatever shape, we have something to work on further and eventually churn out the final draft after a lot of revisions. But, without that first version however disorganized and shabby it may appear, we have made zero progress in writing.

The perfectionist mindset is one major obstacle that often comes in the way of writing the first draft. Apart from the fact that what may be considered a perfect paper is subject to debate and interpretation, the perfectionist approach towards academic writing sets up a very high expectation from ourselves right at the outset. All our mental energy and confidence can become drained in trying to meet those lofty expectations every time we set out to write with very little left to do the actual writing. This leads to a feeling of discouragement and eventual abandonment of our writing project. In summary, the perfectionist mindset doesn't lead to a healthy writing habit.

We need to understand that the healthy pursuit of excellence is helpful and energizing while the striving for artificial standards of perfection is unhealthy and disempowering.

In the field of psychology, there seem to be two major schools of thoughts regarding research on perfectionism. One school believes that any form of perfectionism is problematic, more or less, while the other school differentiates between self-oriented perfectionism that is adaptive and healthy, and maladaptive perfectionism that is pathological or neurotic.

A detailed discussion into the social and cultural causes of perfectionism and the psychological implications is beyond the scope of this book. The author highly recommends the book, *7 Secrets of the Prolific: The Definitive Guide to Overcoming Procrastination, Perfectionism, and Writer's Block*, by Hillary Rettig as it delves deep into the origins of perfectionism and solutions to overcome it at a fundamental level.

For the sake of simplicity, this book distinguishes perfectionism from the healthy traits of "striving for excellence" and uses the following working definition of perfectionism adopted by Fursland et al. (2009): "a pursuit of unrelenting, personally demanding standards, which form the basis of your self-worth and which you pursue despite the huge cost to your wellbeing".

A characteristic symptom of the perfectionist mindset is to set unrealistic goals and standards to measure one's productivity, not only with respect to writing but to all activities. And when they are not met, the perfectionists typically indulge in rebuking themselves with negative labels and remarks such as "sloth", "I must be an idiot", etc.

Quite contrary to the expectation that a perfectionistic approach to writing will result in increased productivity, it actually kills motivation and adds to further procrastination and blocking.

The perfectionists expect a flawless writing environment (the definition of which keeps changing) and have rigid beliefs and notions regarding best writing practices. They often miss the big picture and get picky with the nitty-gritty details. They insist that their first draft should be as good as the final draft since they have already worked out everything in their mind.

The real problem is that perfectionists almost always meet with failure because of setting such self-imposed personally demanding standards that can never be met in reality or can be met only at an enormous cost to themselves. The consequence is that they punish themselves with severe self-critical remarks and thoughts for having failed.

Paul Hewitt, a professor of psychology at the University of British Columbia, Canada who has been conducting research on the treatment of perfectionism for several years, tells an interesting story about one of his patients, a university student who firmly believed that he needed to get an A+ in a course. He studied hard and received an A+ on that course. But, when Hewitt met him afterwards, he found the student to be more depressed and suicidal because the student thought that if he were actually perfect, he wouldn't have had to work so hard to secure the A+ grade! Read this article to learn more about Hewitt's research related to perfectionism: http://goo.gl/ECrbng.

Download the FREE overleaf from this website (http://goo.gl/lLyYMX) that lists some examples of common types of perfectionism behaviors. You can use this as a checklist to observe if you are doing any of the activities mentioned in the list because of setting unrelenting high standards for yourself.

Here are some practical tips on how we can dismantle the striving-for-artificial-perfection mindset and accept a realistic striving-for-excellence mindset in writing:

- Don't think of your thesis, paper or proposal as the next earth-shattering masterpiece. Rather, consider it as a "rough first draft", "write-up", etc. and refer to it as such. Whether or not it will end up being a ground-breaking work (earning thousands of citations) is not something we can determine and is immaterial at the time of writing.

- Accept that "to err is human" and that we all mistakes. No matter how hard we may try, we will still make mistakes. The best part of valor is to learn from our mistakes and not be afraid of making mistakes. This includes learning to make quick decisions on trivial issues (Which font to choose? What design template should I use to get the best results?, etc.), instead of not giving into the 'analysis paralysis'.

- Set your productivity goals (can even be a simple commitment as writing 5 minutes a day) after realistically taking into your consideration other priorities and commitments. Don't try to exponentially increase your writing productivity overnight thinking that your colleague was able to do so.

- Don't judge your output by how great you felt or how bad you felt while writing. In other words, don't judge your output at all. Be satisfied with the effort that you put into writing rather than being preoccupied with some kind of grandiose result that you think is going to come out of it. If you have met your productivity goal for the day, rejoice and congratulate yourself. If not, just wait for tomorrow's turn to try harder. As Hillary Retig nicely puts it, "Learning to recognize and celebrate your successes is a powerful technique for overcoming perfectionism and procrastination."

- By all means, seek social and professional support, feedback and guidance. To seek outside support is not a negative sign of weakness, but a positive sign of courage and a healthy desire to overcome your limiting beliefs that hinder your progress.

YOUR INNER CRITIC

> *"Tell the negative committee that meets inside your head to sit down and shut up."*
>
> *- Ann B. Davis*

❧

Judy Pessmis never took any lead on the few articles that she published during her PhD. Fortunately for her, there were other PhD students and post-docs in her group who were enthusiastically willing to take the lead and do most of the writing. But, now Judy is an assistant professor and she needs papers to get her promotion and tenure. Every time she sits to write her paper, she shudders to think of the final outcome, which in her opinion is going to range anywhere from bad to worse. After she types the first sentence, she says to herself, "Ah! That sentence sucks…only an idiot can write like that".

"I don't think I'll ever be able to write one good paper in my life", she screams at the monitor after she reads the first paragraph that was just completed. Her mind ruminates

over what her colleagues and reviewers may think of her after reading her 'lousy' paper, in her opinion. They may criticize her badly to each other. What if they write to her department Chair to fire her immediately?...

❈

Another major obstacle to free-flowing writing is the defeatist mindset that can range anywhere from indulging in negative self-talk with our mind and with others who espouse a similar approach to developing a deep aversion to writing by repeatedly labeling ourselves with negative adjectives.

It must be now clear that John's perfectionist mindset and Judy's pessimist approach are actually two sides of the same coin. One side projects a very high image of oneself while the other projects a very low image of oneself, with the net effect that both are counter-productive to writing.

Many writers refer to this self-defeating mindset as the "inner critic" or "inner bully" or the "the voice of the oppressor" which is generally associated with some fear of not being able to meet the goals or live up to one's standards. The trick is in discriminating this from the occasional healthy dose of positive and constructive self-criticism aimed towards improvement.

The problem with the inner critic is that it can never be pleased no matter what you do. The more you try to listen to its endless litany and please it, the more it grows stronger and stronger.

Many books and articles have been written on how the inner critic came into being in you and how to tame that inner critic. One practical method advocated by many authors and writing coaches is to separate yourself from your inner critic (which puts on different masks at different times) by being a neutral witness and not participate in any negotiation with it.

Generally, the inner critic's voice is milder in the beginning, but grows louder and louder when you unconsciously struggle to ignore it or when you try to participate in a conversation with it. Instead of doing either, take few deep breath to regain your awareness when your inner critic strikes and note down the first comment it makes on a piece of paper with full consciousness. The inner critic feels indeed gratified that you gave it due importance and eventually quiets down. Take another deep breath and carry on with your writing task.

The breathing exercise and mindful writing slows down your thoughts and puts you in a better position to silence your inner critic. Admittedly, this takes practice, but that is what productive writing is all about!

CHAPTER BIBLIOGRAPHY

Benson, E. (2003). The Many Faces of Perfectionism: The need for perfection comes in different flavors, each associated with its own sets of problems, researchers say. Available at: http://goo.gl/ECrbng.

> *In more than 20 years of research, he [Paul Hewitt, PhD] and his colleagues-- particularly psychologist Gordon Flett, PhD--have found that perfectionism correlates with depression, anxiety, eating disorders and other mental health problems. This summer, several new studies were published that help explain how perfectionism can contribute to psychopathology.*

Brown, B. (2010). The Gifts of Imperfection. Let Go of Who You Think You're Supposed to Be and Embrace Who You are. Hazelden Publishing, Center City, Minnesota.

> *Courage, compassion, and connection seem like big, lofty ideals. But in reality, they are daily practices that, when exercised enough, become these incredible*

gifts in our lives. And the good news is that our vulnerabilities are what force us to call upon these amazing tools. Because we are human and so beautifully imperfect, we get to practice using our tools on a daily basis. In this way, courage, compassion, and connection become gifts—the gifts of imperfection.

Carson, R. (2003). Taming Your Gremlin: A Surprisingly Simple Method for Getting Out of Your Own Way. HarperCollins Publishers, New York, NY.

Your gremlin is the narrator in your head…As you begin to "simply notice" your gremlin, you will become acutely sensitive to the fact that you are not your gremlin, but rather, his observer. You will see clearly that your gremlin has no real hold on you. As this awareness develops, you will begin to appreciate and enjoy your life more and more.

Murray, R. (2009). Writing for Academic Journals. Second Edition. Open University Press, Berkshire, England.

In fact, the dominant characteristic of academic writers is their persistence, as

*much as anything else, which keeps them
going when others give up.*

Rettig, H. (2011). The 7 Secrets of the Prolific: The Definitive Guide to Overcoming Procrastination, Perfectionism, and Writer's Block. First Edition. Infinite Art.

> *The use of shame and coercion as motivational tools, even on yourself, is not just immoral, but futile. They yield not growth and evolution, but, at best, short-term compliance. They also sabotage the creative process.*

Stone, H. and Stone. S. (2011). Embracing Your Inner Critic: Turning Self-Criticism into a Creative Asset. HarperCollins Publishers, San Francisco, CA.

> *The Inner Critic is a self (or subpersonality) that develops to protect us from being shamed or hurt. It is extremely anxious, almost desperate, for us to succeed in the world and to be accepted and liked by others.*

CHAPTER 3
SET SMART GOALS

"Would you please tell me, please which way I ought to go from here?" asked Alice.

That depends on a good deal on where you want to get to," said the Cat.

I don't much care where—" said Alice.

"Then it doesn't matter which way you go," said the Cat.

- Lewis Carroll, Alice's Adventures in Wonderland (2002, p. 53) quoted by O'Neill et al. (2006) in The Power of SMART Goals

❦

One of the main reasons why academic writers aren't productive is because they don't set specific time-bound writing goals before beginning their writing project. Consequently, they get sidetracked somewhere along the way by other topics that interest them or end up, for instance, browsing the internet to find more sources to research and read.

In beginning any writing project, especially the ones that appear to be challenging and vague at the outset, use the concept of SMART goals to break it into small **S**pecific, **M**easurable, **A**ttainable, **R**elevant and **T**ime-bound goals.

The idea of setting SMART goals originated in the field of business management and is often attributed to George T. Doran (1981). Here is an interesting article that traces the history and origins of the SMART objective acronym: http://bit.ly/cRbRmA.

SPECIFIC

Specific goals help you to focus on narrow and concrete tasks that together make up your writing product at the end. As Hillary Rettig notes, Leo Tolstoy didn't write *War and Peace* as one monolithic piece. Rather, he wrote smaller paragraphs and sections that finally combined together to form his magnum opus.

Let us say your writing project is to develop a book on sustainable transportation. Using the SMART goals concept, you first define the final specific outcome of your writing project as: "I will submit the final 500-page manuscript package to the book publisher on August 15th."

Then you work backward to specify narrowed-down, concrete tasks that are relevant to your SMART goal, have a measurable outcome, are achievable, and are time-bound.

A specific task relating to the overall SMART goal in this example may be, for instance, 'to discuss various sustainable modes of transportation and their origins' in the section on Introduction.

You could get more ultra-specific depending on your existing knowledge on the topic. You may need to do some reading and literature review on your topic before you can set specific goals for your project.

Note that to 'write the Introduction' is not a clearly-defined specific goal.

MEASURABLE

Your specific goal should have a measurable outcome as well as metrics that help you assess your progress towards the goal. For instance, you make your specific goal 'to discuss various sustainable modes of transportation and their origins' measurable by specifying the number of pages or words you will devote to this discussion.

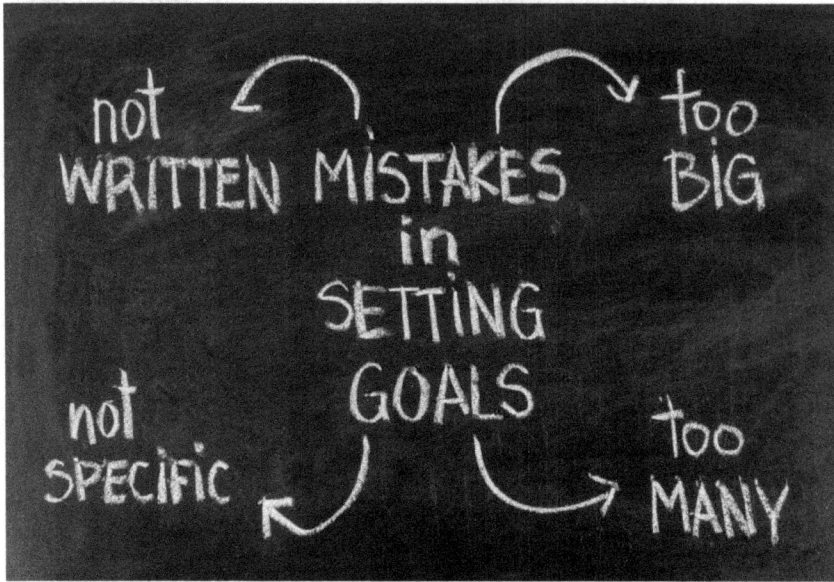

So, your specific and measurable writing goal now is 'to write 4,000 words or 8 pages of discussion on various sustainable modes of transportation and their origins' in the section on Introduction.

ATTAINABLE

Make your specific and measurable goals achievable by realistically taking into consideration other demands on your time and by establishing knowledge-building pathways to fruition. For instance, if you have not read the existing literature on sustainable modes of transport and taken notes, you can't expect to write an 8-page discussion on the sustainable modes of transportation.

The attainable aspect of a SMART goal ensures that you have done your homework to ensure that your specific and measurable writing task is achievable. Thus, 'to write an 8-page discussion on various sustainable modes of transportation and their origins based on the presentation I attended last week' is not an attainable goal whereas 'to write an 8-page discussion on various sustainable modes of transportation and their origins by conducting a state-of-the-art literature review on this topic' is.

RELEVANT

Is what you are researching/reading or writing is relevant to your goal? It typically happens that we start reading or writing on one topic and all of a sudden end up going into a tangent about an item that may not be relevant to the overall topic. For instance, when I research about the sustainable modes of transportation, I discover articles on non-motorized transport and end up reading and writing more pages on this than other sub-topics which is not a desirable outcome (unless you intend it to be that way).

Thus, setting of relevant goals forces you to remain focused on what you want to go into your writing and prevents you from getting sidetracked.

TIME-BOUND

Specific, measurable, attainable, and relevant goals that don't have deadlines are never completed. Set specific deadlines for each of your micro SMART goals that will together constitute your overall SMART goal. This involves both short-term and long-term planning. For instance, we decided in the beginning that our overall SMART goal is that "I will submit the final 500-page manuscript package to the book publisher on August 15th." Now, create multiple micro SMART goals for each of your chapters and sub-sections and tie them to specific timeframes. For instance, "I'll devote 2 hours a day for 7 days to write an 8-page discussion in the Introduction on various sustainable modes of transportation and their origins", etc.

By now you would have realized that setting SMART writing goals is a structured and systematic way to break up a challenging writing project that appears to be vague at the outset into smaller sub-tasks that are specific, measurable, attainable, relevant, and time-bound.

One note of caution that deserves mention here is that while result-focused goals are certainly useful to keep us focused and on our toes, we should not be discouraged by failures in achieving them. For this reason, we should develop more effort-focused goals that place more emphasis on our sincere efforts rather than on the final outcome.

Doran, G. T. (1981). There's a S.M.A.R.T. way to Write Management's Goals and Objectives. Management Review, Vol. 70, No. 11, pp. 35-36.

Klauser, H. A. (2001). Write It Down, Make It Happen: Knowing What You Want – And Getting It! Simon and Schuster, New York, NY.

> *IF YOU KNOW WHAT YOU WANT, YOU CAN HAVE IT. All our years of brain research, all our current knowledge about the corpus callosum, the reticular activating system, and the workings of the human mind, and we are still left with an "aw shucks," "golly gee" sense of wonder that "it works." Write It Down, Make It Happen keeps that sense of winder and is grounded in the same now-scientific truth – that settling your intent, focusing on the outcome, being clear about what you want in life can make your dreams come true.*

O'Neill, J., Conzemius, A., Commodore, C. and Pulsfus, C. (2006). The Power of SMART Goals: Using Goals to Improve Student Learning. Solution Tree Press, Bloomington, IN.

So why do we not use goal-setting and monitoring more pervasively as an improvement method in our schools? Certainly, one big reason is that adopting a goal-conscious state of mind is hard work. It takes time to develop real and compelling goals, and it is even more difficult to make time to continuously monitor progress on goals and then adjust our practices and programs accordingly. Given the current state of most schools where the daily "fires" are attended to and the longer-term "smoldering embers" remain neglected, we are simply not accustomed to a goal-setting habit of mind.

⌘

"I am not a product of my circumstances.
I am a product of my decisions."

- Stephen Covey

⌘

CHAPTER 4
CREATE YOUR DAILY TO-DO LISTS

"Goals are pure fantasy unless you have a specific plan to achieve them."

– Stephen Covey

If you are at loss trying to understand how you spend your time day after day without doing any writing, it is time to start diligently tracking down your activities by the hour. This exercise will help you to identify how your time is consumed and where you can make improvements to open up time for writing.

Do your daily work activities reflect your position responsibilities? Do you spend lot more time preparing for teaching and grading than what is required? May be you have accepted to review too many papers that is not going make a significant difference to your promotion and tenure?

If you are a student, may be you spend too much time on your coursework trying to 'perfect' your home-works and reports with very little time to write? Or every time you sit to write, you end up spending all your time on reading more papers in trying to 'equip' yourself to write?

Take 20-30 minutes on Sunday to plan for the week ahead. A little planning can go a long way in ensuring that our daily writing goal is accomplished with minimal stress. Remember one of the findings from Boice's study: lack of planning leads to stressful binge writing accompanied by unhealthy euphoric states and high error rates in writing.

For most of us, the week ahead may be more or less clear in terms of what we need to accomplish: teaching/course schedule is fixed, review requests always come with deadlines, we get regular e-mail reminders about when the research reports are due, we have already penciled in the deadlines for submitting the proposals or conference paper abstracts or book chapters or articles to a special issue.

Of course, there are always emergencies, some which we can plan for and others that are beyond our control.

Based on the weekly plan you have developed, create a To-Do list for every day in the week and include it in your weekly calendar. This makes it easier to do a quick review of the To-Do list for the day and update, if necessary, the first thing in the morning. The power of creating a simple To-Do list cannot be underestimated.

Always remember one thing: no matter how expert you become at time management and no matter how much more time you can squeeze out of a day, you are never going to catch up. Too much to do and too little time to do them in.

Especially, in academia, your responsibilities keep increasing higher and higher. New tasks and deadlines keep getting added to your list as you struggle to complete the existing ones.

So, all we can do is to be selective, set clear priorities and focus on completing the most important tasks. As Brian Tracy, the author of international bestseller, *Eat That Frog!: 21 Great Ways to Stop Procrastinating and Get More Done in Less Time*, notes, "The ability to concentrate single-mindedly on your most important task, to do it well and to finish it completely, is the key to great success, achievement, respect, status, and happiness in life".

You can create a To-Do list whichever way you want. Some use online apps such as the Todoist while others use the MS Outlook to create their lists. I still prefer the use of a pen and paper to list all the tasks for the day (with the most important ones on the top including writing) and striking off each activity as it is completed. This builds confidence and a sense of accomplishment which are important for a productive rest-of-the-day.

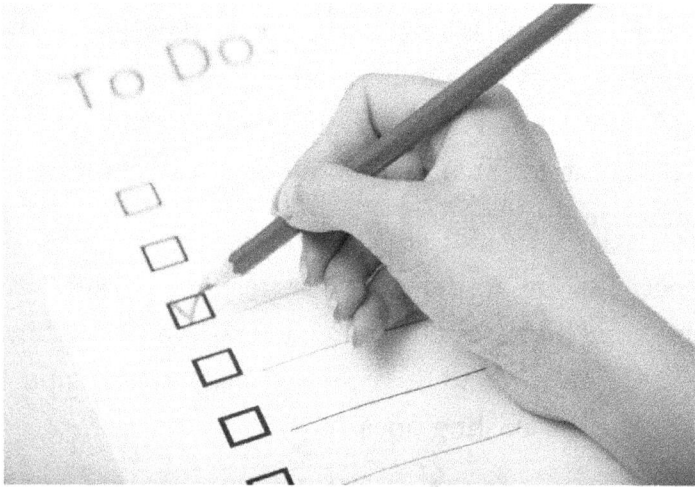

CHAPTER 5
WRITE DAILY

"Sow a thought and you reap an action; sow an act and you reap a habit; sow a habit and you reap a character; sow a character and you reap a destiny."

– *Ralph Waldo Emerson*

We all know by experience that anything we do on a daily basis has a remarkable effect on our overall well-being than those activities we do sporadically or once in a while. This is true even for simple activities like exercising, spending time with family, etc.

We only have 16-18 useful hours in a day and we have to spend it wisely between our personal and professional lives. And once the daily clock starts, you can't pause it. Time and tide wait for none. So, we really can't manage time, we can only manage our priorities.

The single most useful writing advice offered by almost all productive writers and writing coaches is this: write daily!

As author Jane Hyatt Yolen advises, "Exercise the writing muscle every day, even if it is only a letter, notes, a title list, a character sketch, a journal entry. Writers are like dancers, like athletes. Without that exercise, the muscles seize up".

Someone may say, "I get my writing done anyway under the pressure of a looming deadline. And proposals and papers always have deadlines. So, what's the big deal?" Well, we already have enough anxieties and uncertainties in our lives to worry about. So, why to add more to the list?

Also, as we have seen from Boice's study, this reactive binge-writing mode is not only unfulfilling, but it also puts a lot of stress on our system and doesn't helps us to develop good writing habits with stable and sustained productivity.

Previous as well as contemporary research tells us that the most productive writers are those who write daily in small chunks of time.

Charles Duhigg, a reporter for the New York Times and the author of the New York Times Bestseller, *The Power of Habit: Why We Do What We Do in Life and Business* examines in his book why habits exist. When we examine our lives, we realize that most of our daily routine is simply made up of habits, good or bad.

At one point in life, we made certain conscious choices with respect to all of our daily actions (how much to sleep, what to eat and what not to eat, when to check e-mail, etc.). Those actions became automatic after some time and evolved into habits. His conclusion is that "habits can be changed, if we understand how they work."

The relevance of Duhigg's book to productive writing is that when we make a conscious choice to write daily, we are forming a life-long healthy habit.

The Artist Way, a movement inspired by author Julia Cameron's idea, has popularized Morning Pages, a concept where you write three pages of unedited freewriting or stream-of-consciousness writing first thing in the morning daily. Obviously, what you write in the Morning Pages is not meant to be published, but it is to help you kick-start your writing engine first thing in the morning, get your thoughts out on paper, and get your ideas flowing throughout the day. This seemed to have helped many authors develop a healthy writing habit.

WHEN TO WRITE?

> *"It is by sitting down to write every morning that one becomes a writer."*
>
> *– Gerald Brenan*

❇

First, let us consider the benefits of doing our writing in the morning. That's when our mind is fresh and clear after a good night's sleep and that's the time our creative juices are flowing. And when you get your writing done in the morning and strike it off of your To-Do list, you gain confidence that carries you through the rest of the day. More importantly, it reinforces your desire to achieve your writing goals.

A number of research studies have been conducted on studying the brain patterns and neuron connections at different times of the day to answer this question: are there specific times of the day that are more suited than other times to get certain things done? Skipping all the technical details, the answer is 'yes'! This body of research does point to the fact that morning time is the best when it comes to writing especially if you are looking for creativity.

There is another way to look at this. We all know that we have limited reserves of will power. Studies have shown we have limited reserves of will power and that it tends to get drained when faced with successively challenging tasks, even if they are of completely different nature (Baumeister and Tierney 2011).

So, we do want to leverage our willpower to facilitate the writing process, especially on those days when we don't feel like writing at all. As the day progresses, our willpower is consumed by multiple stressors in the form of teaching, field visit, a stressful phone call, disturbing e-mails, etc. So, it makes sense to use the morning time when our willpower is supposed to be at its peak to gain momentum in our writing.

There is also a large body of research that shows that creative part of our brain is most active during sleep and right after sleep. On the other hand, the analytical part of our brain (which we want to harness for editing and proofreading tasks) is most active as the day goes by.

Studies have looked at the Magnetic Resonance Imaging (MRI) scans of the brain and have concluded that our creativity is at its peak in the mornings. This seems to make sense as we all have the experience of running into brilliant ideas and inspirations when we are taking our morning shower (and run out of the bathroom shouting 'Eureka'!). This doesn't mean that you can't tap into your creativity at other times of the day.

So, if our creativity and willpower are at their zenith during the early morning hours, then that's when our writing time should be scheduled.

Now, someone may say, "Well, guess what? I'm not a morning person, but more of an evening person and that's when my efficiency is high and that's when I get things get done". That's certainly possible.

It is also possible that some may have chronic ailments that do not allow them to function efficiently in the morning or that they find it impossible to include even 30 minutes of writing into their daily morning schedule. Not a big deal. In that case, it is highly suggested that we write at a specific time every day so that we get into a consistent writing routine.

For instance, it is said that Charles Dickens would write in the morning and complete all his writing by 2 PM whereas Robert Frost would start his writing sometime around 2 PM and write throughout the night. But, they had one thing in common when it came to their writing schedule. They achieved productivity by following the same writing routine day after day.

Cognitive scientists agree that our neural connections are strengthened and reinforced by anything we do consistently as a routine or a habit. So, following a daily writing regimen is good irrespective of whether you are a morning lark, night owl, or a daytime hummingbird.

USE FREEWRITING

> *"You can sit there, tense and worried, freezing the creative energies, or you can start writing something. It doesn't matter what. In five or ten minutes, the imagination will heat, the tightness will fade, and a certain spirit and rhythm will take over."*
>
> *- Leonard Bernstein*

One may say, "I don't have anything to write daily". It doesn't matter. What we are trying to cultivate is this positive habit of daily writing. We want to get accustomed to this notion that no matter what else we may do or not do, we can't skip writing. So, even if you feel you don't have anything significant to write on a given day, just write because you have to write.

Write about a concocted research study that investigates the feelings and experiences of individuals while they are commuting from home to work. Write a cover letter for the dream job you want to apply to. Write whatever you feel like. If you don't feel like writing, ask yourself why and write the answers. You get the point.

Peter Elbow offers the following advice on freewriting in his famous book, *Writing Without Teachers*:

> *Don't stop for anything. Go quickly without rushing. Never stop to look back, to cross something out, to wonder how to spell something, to wonder what word or thought to use, or to think about what you are doing. If you can't think of a word or a spelling, just use a squiggle or else write "I can't think what to say, I can't think what to say" as many times as you want;*

or repeat the last word you wrote over and
over again; or anything else. The only
requirement is that you never stop.

Employ the freewriting technique to get your messy first draft and save editing for the future drafts. As Henriette Anne Klauser, the author of *Writing on Both Sides of The Brain: Breakthrough Techniques for People Who Write* notes, "the work habit that underlies virtually all writing problems is the tendency to write and edit simultaneously".

If you feel severely blocked, this is how you can use the five-minute freewriting technique to your advantage. Make a determination that all you need to do is to show up at the scheduled time to write for five minutes. In the beginning, even if you don't feel like writing, simply show up at the scheduled time, sit in your chair and start writing.

Use the freewriting advice (available for FREE download at http://goo.gl/7DIvFX) offered by Peter Elbow to keep writing for five minutes, no matter what.

Reward yourself at the end of your five-minute scheduled writing session. Once you feel familiar and comfortable with the five-minute freewriting technique, you will be able to gradually increasing your writing stints to longer durations.

For most academicians, writing 30 minutes a day seems to be an achievable goal.

WRITING IS THINKING

> *"I write entirely to find out what I'm thinking, what I'm looking at, what I see and what it means. What I want and what I fear."*
>
> – *Joan Didion*

It is very tempting to think that the writing component, whether you are working on a thesis or a paper or a proposal, comes in the end after you have completed your research and figured out everything in your head clearly. But, this is not actually true.

If you wait to write until you are perfectly clear about what you want to write, it may never get done.

To become productive and effective academic writers, we should change the paradigm from "thinking in order to write" to "writing in order to think". In other words, writing is thinking.

Think of writing as a medium to have an ongoing dialogue with your thinking self, a way to catalyze your critical thinking process. Thoughts become more concrete and focused when you put pen to paper or finger to keyboard.

Approach writing as an engaging way of raising questions about your research or the topic you want to write about, as a tool to raise interesting arguments and seek answers to your questions, and as a medium to vent out your daily frustrations.

After developing your messy first draft using the freewriting technique, it is time to engage your "editing" part of the brain to clean up and flesh out ideas by raising appropriate questions and looking for connections to revise your draft further and further.

Once you have successfully developed a structured outline for your work, it is easier to make further progress as it enables you to "shift around" in writing different sections in any order rather than writing linearly with the possibility of getting stuck.

When Isaac Asimov was asked, "What if you get a writer's block?", he said, "I don't ever get one precisely because I switch from one task to another at will. If I'm tired of one project, I just switch to something else which, at that moment, interests me more."

As you make progress from the first draft to final draft, it is helpful to print out what you have written and read it aloud. Hearing your own writing is the best way to tell if your writing is active, has a flow to it, as well as to discern proper punctuation. This is also an opportunity to get both experts and non-experts to review your manuscript.

CHAPTER BIBLIOGRAPHY

Baumeister, R. F. and Tierney, J. (2011). Willpower: Rediscovering the Greatest Human Strength. The Penguin Press, New York, NY.

Boice (1989). Procrastination, Busyness and Bingeing. Behavioral Research Therapy, Vol. 27, No. 6, pp. 605-611.

> *The evidence here suggests that new professors doing writing in brief daily sessions, especially when they allowed external prods to motivate them, were far more productive as writers than were their colleagues who continued to write on more traditional schedules..*

Elbow P. (1998). Writing with Power: Techniques for Mastering the Writing Process. Second Edition. Oxford University Press, New York, NY.

Klauser, H. A. (1987). Writing on Both Sides of the Brain: Breakthrough Techniques for People Who Write. Harper Collins Publishers, New York, NY.

> *The challenge is to learn how to unlock the Ariel part of you at will and to train*

yourself to keep Caliban quiet until called upon to comment – first to write fluently and well, and then to invite the critical faculty back, as your guest, to sit down with you in a nonjudgmental, helpful way, look over what you have written, and make suggestions for improvement, without name calling, without beating down.

CHAPTER 6
SET A TIMER WHEN YOU WRITE

"Lost time is never found again"

– Benjamin Franklin

I want you to do a simple exercise. Take an activity that you normally do during your work day – say reading a research article. Note down the time you start and the time you complete studying it. For argument sake, let us say it took you 45 minutes. Now, pick up another research article that is of similar length and complexity compared to the first one and say to yourself that you have to finish studying this in the next 30 minutes.

Did you notice any difference in your focus between the two endeavors? You'll surely find that your focus and productivity is much higher when you have to get something done within a specific time interval than when you have all the time to get it done.

The reason why it works is because you start holding yourself accountable and responsible for how you spend your time. Accountability is a key principle to improving our productivity and performance, especially when it comes to writing. We'll talk about this in detail in a later chapter.

When we start using a timer to get things done at work, the first thing we'll realize is that we have been spending more time on things that ought to take less of our time. Anything that eats away our time, including spending hours and hours preparing for teaching, at the cost of no writing for the day is not worth it because a significant portion of what really matters for our academic career success and reputation is our writing productivity.

There are many stopwatch and timer apps and software available both for online and offline use. For Windows, the following timer applications seem to be popular owing to their simplicity:

- Orzeszek Timer (**Free**)

- Focus Booster (**Free**)

- CookTimer (**Free**)

For Mac users, the Timer for Mac application is the most popular.

As mentioned before, developing the healthy habit of writing in small chunks of time daily goes a long way in achieving the goal of steady and sustained productivity. Many authors and writers have found the Pomodoro Technique to be useful in this regard.

Unless you have already established consistent and steady levels of daily writing output, it is a good idea to stop when the timer goes off. This will ensure that you don't get into the euphoric binge-writing mode on days you feel super-excited about writing which can't be sustained even the very next day.

First, establish a regulated daily writing routine (30 minutes a day is good to begin with) and then gradually increase it as you go along, if needed. Don't forget to give yourself a treat (can be as simple as taking a walk, but something that you enjoy) as it positively reinforces your writing habit.

THE POMODORO TECHNIQUE

The Pomodoro Technique is a time valuing and management technique developed by Francesco Cirillo in the late 1980s that helps you to break down a big task into small sub-tasks using a timer. How?

Break down the time it will take for a massive task to be accomplished into small time intervals (typically 25 minutes in length) followed by short breaks. After four pomodori (plural for pomodoro), you get the reward of a longer break, anywhere from 15-30 minutes.

The idea behind the Pomodoro Technique (named after the tomato-shaped kitchen timer that Cirillo first used as a University student; 'pomodoro' means tomato in Italian) is that small periods of focused effort with no distractions and lots of breaks improves the mental agility and helps us to become more productive rather than adopting a bite-all-at-once approach.

An added benefit of this technique is that by doing some physical work (such as getting up from your chair and running in the same place or doing jumping jacks) during those small breaks helps you to stay physically fit. This is especially important for us academicians who are prone to a sedentary lifestyle. A number of freely downloadable and installable time-management apps are available based on the Pomodoro Technique:

- ORANGE time management for iPhone and iPad apps

- Flowkeeper for PC users

- PomodorApp for Mac users

- ClearFocus for Android phones

The Pomodoro Technique is just one time management technique that can be applied not only to writing but to any task at work.

Choose and use what works for you the best, but the most important thing is to stay in your chair and write during your scheduled time to reach your daily word-count goal. If it is that you find the Pomodoro

Technique or any of the time management strategies too complex or that they are interfering with your writing, it is best that you skip them rather than skipping your writing.

Write or Die (http://writeordie.com/) is an interesting web application to get you jump started on writing if it is that you find yourself analyzing too much what to write and how to write. Originally designed with an aim to eliminate writer's block with threatening consequences for procrastination, it provides you with a distraction-free web space to write your text and uses negative reinforcements to stimulate your writing, forcing you to meet your writing goal.

With Write or Die, you get to set your word count and the time duration as well as how you want the app to 'remind' you if you stop writing. The negative consequences of not writing for too long could range from a gentle pop-up text box or an annoying sound or worse, your written words start disappearing one by one.

In the most recent version (Write or Die 2), the app allows you to set rewards for your accomplishment such as the appearance of pleasing images after you have met a specified word count. Many fiction as well as non-fiction authors have found this app to be useful to instantly break free from the heavy inertia that often holds us from putting our thoughts to the paper or the screen.

Have you come across situations where you really find it hard to explain or paraphrase, in your own words, a concept that you read in a paper or a book? One simple solution is to record your speech and transcribe it. You could make short notes as you read along and then speak out your understanding into a voice recorder or use a speech recognition software. Alternatively, you could prepare a PPT and record your speech as you present it to an imagined friend sitting next to you.

Instead of purchasing a costly speech recognition software, you could use a free online app like Dictation (https://dictation.io) that "internally uses the built-in speech recognition engine of Google Chrome to transform your voice into digital text".

Monitor Your Output

Tracking your writing progress is beneficial in many ways. All control systems and best management practices include a feedback loop to identify anomalies and to improve the system performance.

The amount of writing you do per day (word count or number of pages) and for what duration is very much quantifiable and something that helps you to identify patterns, the things that you did before and after which impacted your writing goal for the day, how close or far you are with respect to completing your writing project at this rate and so on.

In other words, monitoring your writing output on a weekly basis helps you to identify and reinforce healthy writing habits and avoid habits that lead to reduced writing productivity.

You can choose the traditional pen-and-paper method or an Excel spreadsheet or a software like RescueTime to accurately track how you spend your work day. Are you spending too much time on an activity that interests you, but not relevant to your goals? What are the big time consumers on your daily schedule? When can you schedule your daily writing session that you can realistically commit to?

Tracking your writing output gives you a valuable set of data that you can use to mine all sorts of Qs & As to improve your writing productivity.

Chapter Bibliography

Zerubavel, E. (2001). The Clockwork Muse: A Practice Guide to Writing Theses, Dissertations, and Books. Harvard University Press, Cambridge, MA.

> *It is methodicalness and routinization that help us produce theses, dissertations, and books. And it is the time schedule and the timetable that help us bring them into our writing.*

⌘

"*Concentrate all your thoughts upon the work at hand. The sun's rays do not burn until brought to a focus.".*"

- Alexander Graham Bell

⌘

CHAPTER 7
ELIMINATE DISTRACTIONS

*"Work is hard. Distractions are plentiful.
And time is short."*

- Adam Hochschild

✂

The importance of a good, distraction-free, interruption-free environment for writing cannot be understated. Distractions can have external or internal origins, but how we choose to respond to those distractions always rests with us.

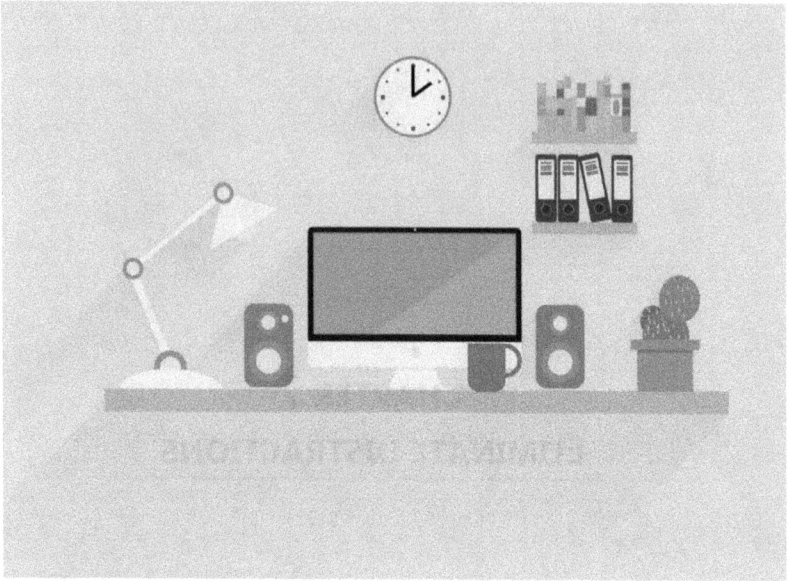

Avoid Online Distractions

OK, I do understand the value of forming the healthy habit of daily writing with a consistent routine. I see the benefits that can come from writing in small chunks of time rather than sporadic outbursts of binge writing. I have even managed to 'stick my butt in the chair', as they say, with an aim to achieve my writing goal for the day. My fingers are poised over the keyboard and I am ready to type...Wait! I need to update my Facebook chat status to 'offline' so that nobody can disturb me while I write.

I go to Facebook and find that someone has shared an interesting post on productivity hacks. Impulsively, I click on it...and there goes my resolution to write for the day. After spending 30 minutes of reading related articles and reader's comments on productivity hacks, I discover that I have procrastinated my writing to get lost in the online labyrinth. How many of us have had similar experiences almost on a daily basis (or should we say hourly basis)?

Facebook is just one example. Did you know that an average American spends 3+ hours a day social networking from a computer, tablet, and/or mobile phone. According to one recent report, adults in the US spent almost 30 hours using apps on their Smartphones every month by the end of 2013, a 65% increase from what it was at the end of 2011. This includes long stretches of time spent on those apps or simply unlocking the phones to text/e-mail or for social networking.

The point is that it may not be Facebook or Twitter, but some other 'online trap' that is waiting to consume our time. We don't even discover it in the beginning when we casually enter the online globe. By the time we realize it, we are deeply entangled into a web of links, videos, and pictures and finally get out of it often with an empty feeling. The term 'world wide web' seems very appropriate. This is not to say that anything online is bad, but experience tells us that we end up spending a lot more time than intended if we are not careful and purposeful while going online.

From the productivity perspective, we do want to eliminate all distractions while writing including the temptation to go online even to read a research article or lookup something. Academic writing is a non-linear process where the activities of studying/researching and writing proceed in parallel often times.

For instance, if you are presenting some arguments while writing a grant proposal or a journal article, you may want to first put down your arguments and then look for references/sources to substantiate your arguments. Even if that's the case, it is best not to interrupt your flow while writing because it becomes increasingly difficult to get back into the flow when there are unintended breaks.

The best way to deal with online nuisance is to simply unplug the Ethernet cable or to turn off the Wi-Fi before you start to write.

If you are not comfortable with that, there are a number of apps that can temporarily block out your access to certain web sites that you specify. These include:

- SelfControl for Mac Users

- Leechblock – **An add-on for Firefox users**

- Nanny for Google Chrome – An add-on for Chrome users

It can be distracting to keep all sorts of programs open while you write, especially your e-mail program.

Working on your e-mails the first thing in the morning is the best way to guarantee an unproductive rest-of-the-day. And, nowadays we have multiple e-mail accounts to worry about.

Instead of doing emails, get your day to a great start by finishing one important task on your to-do list. I hope that task would be same on all workdays, i.e., to write for 30 minutes. Completing this important task will not only boost your confidence, but will help you to get your thoughts more organized and focused.

Even many senior faculty members and administrators in the academic environment with lots of responsibilities have been able to be productive by checking e-mails just once a day, even during crunch time!

Disabling new e-mail notifications and alerts and setting our office and personal phones to silent mode or at least beep mode are some simple favors we can do unto ourselves before we set out to write. There will always be some exceptional circumstances some days where your writing is interrupted by some emergency situation needing your immediate attention.

But, at least from our side, we can do everything humanly possible in creating a distraction-free and conducive writing environment. Needless to say that a clean, well-lit, and organized writing space helps you to remain calm and focused.

GET INTERNAL FOCUS AND CALMNESS

"The point of power is always in the present moment."

- Louise L. Hay

✤

Ah! that meeting killed all my time...I have so many things left on my To-Do list...John must be stupid to talk to me like that. The next time he meets me, I'll teach him a lesson. If he becomes upset, I'll give him a piece of my mind. Who do you think I am? Ah! that smell reminds me of the pizza we ate last weekend. I am looking forward to the next weekend...football game on Saturday, rock concert on Sunday...what a relief! I don't know what they did with all my books stored in the attic of grandma's house...I have so much reading to do before I can start this paper...

Sounds familiar?

This is just a snapshot of the non-stop chatter we are constantly subjected to day in and day out by our inseparable partner, the mind. It is never tired of giving a running commentary and rambling on and on. Every impression we come across is registered by the ever-vigilant mind and stored in an expandable repository to be pulled out and presented to us in the future at the most unexpected moment.

Even at night after we are fast asleep, the mind stays awake making plans, regurgitating the events of the day, mixing and matching ideas, people, places, past, present and future and allowing us to experience its motley presentation in the form of dreams.

By now, you must have gotten a sense of how important it is to quieten the mind from distracting thoughts to focus on the writing. The internal distractions are far more difficult to deal with than the external ones.

Here, we are not talking about the 'inner critic' (which was addressed in Chapter 2), but the rambling, disoriented thoughts that keeps distracting us from focusing on any one objective. It takes us swiftly from one thought to another, and from one continent to another in less than a moment's notice.

Because of an unfocussed mind, we either judgmentally dwell in the past ("I wish I could have started this paper a month earlier. What a lazy person!") or wildly speculate about the future ("How nice it will be if I can get that best paper award for this paper"), but never live in the present ("Let me write this sentence down").

There could be a number of reasons why our mind is unsettled, including anxiety, stress, lack of adequate sleep, improper diet, etc. Whatever the reason may be, the result is that an unfocussed mind severely hampers our productivity.

Of course, often times an unfulfilled obligation such as "today is the last day to pay the rent for this month" may keep popping up throughout the day. The best way to deal with it is to jot it down on a paper (and put a time next to it when you'll attend to it) and continue with your writing.

Psychologists agree that our voluntary attention to a task at hand cannot be sustained over long period of time, but that it gradually wanes over time, a phenomenon referred to as 'vigilance decrement'.

Studies have demonstrated that some sort of training or repetitive practice can improve performance in vigilance tasks. There is a growing body of evidence that suggests that daily practice of meditation (even as little as 10 minutes per day) can actually help improve our focus and concentration. Research has also demonstrated that prayers can help prevent cognitive depletion.

One study conducted by researchers at the University of California, Davis (MacLean et al. 2010) shows that long-term meditation can help people focus their attention and sustain it, even during the most boring of tasks.

Meditation doesn't necessarily mean some complex routine practiced atop the Himalayas. It can be as simple as *consciously* taking few deep breaths every hour or so at your desk. This slows down your racing thoughts and brings back the focus to the present moment – *the now*.

Recently, there has been an explosion of interest in the practice of "mindfulness" meditation as a means of achieving overall well-being, including tuning out unwanted distractions. According to Jon-Kobat Zinn, the founder and director of the Stress Reduction Clinic and the creator of the Center for Mindfulness at the University of Massachusetts (UMass) Medical School, "mindfulness is awareness, cultivated by paying attention in a sustained and particular way: on purpose, in the present moment, and non-judgmentally".

A number of research studies conducted in the US at the Center for Mindfulness at the UMass Medical School, The Greater Good Science at University of California-Berkeley, and The Center for Investigating Health Minds at the University of Wisconsin-Madison document the physical, psychological, and social benefits of mindfulness meditation.

CHAPTER BIBLIOGRAPHY

Boice, R. (1997). Which is More Productive, Writing in Binge Patterns of Creative Illness or in Moderation? Written Communication, Vol. 14, No. 4, pp. 435-459.

Hammerness, P. and Moore, M. (20120). Train Your Brain to Focus. Available at: http://goo.gl/LxZ8kC.

> *To prevent distractions from hijacking your focus, use the ABC method as your brain's brake pedal. Become Aware of your options: you can stop what you are doing and address the distraction, or you can let it go. Breathe deeply and consider your options. Then Choose thoughtfully: Stop? or Go?*

Kabat-Zinn, J. (2011). Mindfulness for Beginners: Reclaiming the Present Moment—and Your Life. Sounds True, Boulder, CO.

Kabat-Zinn, J. (2013). Full Catastrophe Living: Using the Wisdom of Your Body and Mind to Face Stress, Pain, and Illness. Revised Edition. Random House, LLC, New York, NY.

MacLean et al. (2010). Intensive Meditation Training Improves Perpetual Discrimination and Sustained Attention. Psychological Science, Vol. 21, No. 6, pp. 829-839.

MarketingCharts Staff (2013). Social Networking Eats Up 3+ Hours Per Day for The Average American User. Available at: http://goo.gl/MMzO5N.

Carr, N. (2008). Is Google Making Us Stupid? Available at: http://goo.gl/AYKRk.

> *It is clear that users are not reading online in the traditional sense; indeed there are signs that new forms of "reading" are emerging as users "power browse" horizontally through titles, contents pages and abstracts going for quick wins. It almost seems that they go online to avoid reading in the traditional sense....[Quoted from a recently published study of online research habits conducted by scholars from University College London]*

CHAPTER 8
BE ACCOUNTABLE

"Accountability breeds response-ability."

– Stephen Covey

❋

Unfortunately, that which has the highest bearing on our academic career and professional success, either as a graduate student, post-doc or tenure-track professor, gets the least priority. You know what I am talking about, right?

Writing.

But, Why?

Because it has the least built-in accountability, says Kerry Ann Rocquermore, President of the National Center for Faculty Development and Diversity (NCFDD). She refers to this as the "structural challenge of the faculty work" and goes on to say that "the most important factor in your promotion has the least accountability". The consequence of this is that we always find excuses to avoid it, resist it and postpone it.

It is just human nature to neglect those activities that don't yield pleasurable reward and keep engaging in those that do, irrespective of how important or unimportant they are for our actual well-being.

The most common example we can give in this regard is related to physical fitness. Everyone knows that some sort of daily exercise goes a long way to help us stay fit. But, not everyone finds it pleasurable and may even consider it a waste of time. So, we neglect it by giving it a low priority.

Similarly, we may keep postponing writing giving it a low priority by busily engaging ourselves in other activities. After some time, we may even start justifying that we are unable to invest time in writing because we are very busy with other things.

Is there a way to break free from this self-deception by being accountable to ourselves or having someone hold us accountable for our writing?

Rewarding ourselves abundantly after completing our scheduled writing session is the best form of self-accountability, according to Boice who refers to this as "contingency management". The idea behind this is to associate your writing with a pleasurable reward of your choice (go for a walk, listen to music, etc.) such that gradually the writing itself becomes the reward.

As Joan Bolker, the author of *Writing Your Dissertation in Fifteen Minutes a Day*, says, "positive reinforcement, rewarding ourselves each step of the way as we accomplish a series of small goals on the way to achieving the large one, is both more pleasant and much more effective".

Apart from self-accountability, we may also need the help of a writing coach or a writing pal/buddy - someone who can regularly check on us everyday or every few days and promptly ask for updates on our writing.

Contrary to the popular belief that shutting ourselves up in isolation and writing can improve productivity, research related to faculty development has shown that accountability and support can actually help achieve sustainable and steady levels of productivity.

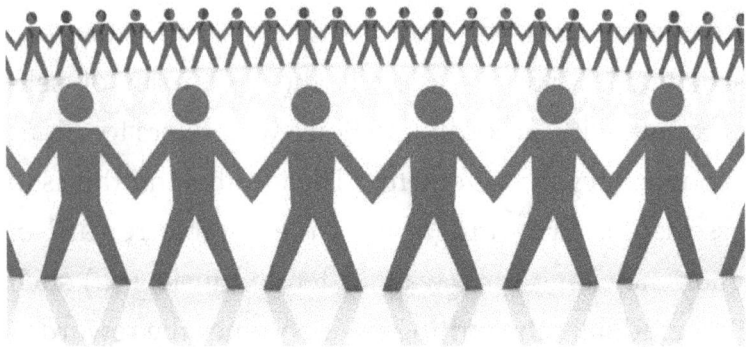

The words accountability and support may conjecture a mental image where we have to come to fully depend on someone to help with our writing, somewhat like a parasite! Far from that crippling notion, the idea here is to encourage active feedback and synergistic exchange of experience with a writing partner or a writing group to make writing not only a productive, but also a pleasurable experience.

We may need the help of a real writing partner like a colleague across the hall with whom we can have face-to-face contact and live discussions to motivate ourselves to write regularly.

Most universities have an academic writing center that you can seek support and feedback from, if you are a student. They have dedicated staff and writing tutors who can sit with you and discuss your writing needs and guide you through the writing process. I highly recommend this option to students as it is free and the kind of support and feedback you'll receive especially if you are writing your thesis or dissertation is highly useful.

Note that the university writing center staff will not offer to re-write your entire manuscript nor can they provide any discipline-specific technical input to improve the quality of your writing. But, they are well-qualified and trained to guide you through the writing process from the standpoint of form, structure and flow and help you to overcome thinking and writing blocks. They are generally willing to meet with you week after week to check on your writing progress and hold you accountable (if you want them to). Isn't that a great resource?

Someone at the university writing center may also be able to help you in establishing your own small writing support group comprised of 6 to 7 individuals. There are many advantages to having a support group like that.

Apart from the primary benefit of helping you to become more accountable, a writing group offers you the opportunity to connect with other writers functioning in a similar environment as you. It can help you overcome feelings of frustration, isolation and shame that can often come in the way of productive writing.

As Wendy Laura Belcher, the author of *Writing Your Journal Article in 12 Weeks: A Guide to Academic Publishing Success*, says, "Writing is, after all, a creative process and like any such process, depends on connection. If you try to create in an environment where sharing is discouraged, dysfunction is the inevitable result. Certainly, many have found that talking about their struggles with writing has been very freeing, both for them and for their chosen confidant. The lesson: Learning to talk about writing is an important key to becoming a productive writer."

After establishing some trust and friendship with your writing group, you have the company of other writers who understand your constraints and struggles, who can empathize with your situation and are even willing to put some pressure on you to get the writing done, when needed. It is very much possible that someone in the group may already have found their way out of a specific obstacle that you are beginning to experience, thus saving you tons and tons of time in having to reinvent the wheel.

In her popular book, *Writing Your Dissertation in Fifteen Minutes a Day,* Joan Bolker discusses at length the pros and cons, issues to be considered, problems, expectations and setting up goals and parameters in creating your own writing group.

Some may prefer the comfort of a virtual writing group that doesn't expect you to leave your office or reveal your identity. There are many free or fee-based online writing groups that could help us to stay on course.

The NCFDD is "an independent professional development, training, and mentoring community of over 71,000 graduate students, post-docs, and faculty members".

You can join NCFDD either as an individual or an institutional member. Their paid membership benefits include free access to online/on-campus writing workshops, webinars, discussion forums, professional development training, and intensive mentoring programs.

Similarly, the Academic Writing Club is a fee-based online accountability-based coaching system (starting price of $97 for one 4-week session) that "helps you to develop ideal writing habits" and improve your writing productivity by working with an academic coach and a small group of peers.

As a member of the Academic Writing Club, you get to report on your daily writing struggles and accomplishments to the coach and a small group of peers who can offer feedback and support and hold you accountable for your writing goals.

CHAPTER BIBLIOGRAPHY

Belcher, W. L. (2009). Writing Your Journal Article in 12 Weeks: A Guide to Academic Publishing Success. Sage Publications, Thousand Oaks, CA.

> *Nothing is as collaborative as good writing. All texts depend on other texts, all writers stand on the shoulders of other writers, all prose demands an editor, and all writing needs an audience. Without community, writing is inconceivable.*

Boice, R. (1982). Increasing the Writing Productivity of 'Blocked' Academicians. Behavior Research Therapy, Vol. 20, pp. 197-207.

> *He [referring to Wallace (1979)] describes how he eventually discovered, despite the romantic notions implanted by society, that writers become successful not through flashes of inspiration but by dint of hard and uniform labor. Wallace, who 'creates discipline' by keeping charts of his daily output of writing reports pleasure in the discovery that other geniuses have 'stooped' to use similar devices as spurs to*

writing. The suggestion...is that record keeping and other methodical procedures can be used to treat writers who complain of unproductiveness (Goldiamond, 1977).

Rocquemore, K. A. (2010). Shut Up and Write. Inside Higher Ed. Available at: http://bit.ly/1IKGY5f.

While it should go without saying, it's OK to have needs. In fact, if you wait until you are perfectly motivated, flawlessly self-disciplined, free from anxiety, utterly fearless, intellectually energized, and emotionally resolved before you start writing this summer, you may never begin! Instead, I want to encourage you to release yourself from the idea that having needs means there's something wrong with you. It's OK if you need support and accountability.

CHAPTER 9
WRAP UP

"Great is the art of beginning, but greater is the art of ending."

- Henry Wadsworth Longfellow

❃

We have come a long way from where we started.

We saw how our limiting beliefs and accepting the common myths about writing can interfere with our productivity and discussed some practical tips on overcoming them.

We talked about setting SMART goals and developing a weekly plan and daily To-Do lists that puts writing as one of the topmost priorities.

We highlighted the use of freewriting technique to write a lot and produce the messy first draft and use writing as a "lens to focus one's mind" to do revisions.

We discussed the importance of setting a timer while we write and monitoring our daily output as a means of improving our productivity.

Finally, we talked about the benefits of self- and external accountability to overcome feelings of isolation, exchange and learn new ideas, socialize and connect with other writers to actively seek mutual support, feedback, and guidance – an important trait of productive academic writers.

Here is a summary of the most important principles, tips and strategies we have covered in this book:

Introduction

- Academic writing is admittedly hard work from conception to completion.

- There are various kinds of disempowering blocks academic writers experience that hold them from achieving steady and sustained levels of writing productivity. Perfectionism, procrastination, lack of accountability, and other hindrances ranging from emotional to mental to physical blocks have been identified as the major causes for unproductive writing.

- Multiple lines of empirical evidence supported by a large body of research are suggestive of the following key strategies for producing low-stress prolific writing: freewriting, writing on a schedule, positive reinforcement of healthy writing habits, making oneself accountable to a writing buddy or a small group of writers in similar situations (which also offers the opportunity to have your writing critiqued by experts and non-experts).

- Productive academic writers carry out their essential activities, including writing, in small chunks of time, rather than adopting a deadline-driven binge mode of operation.

- Anyone aspiring to become a productive academic writer can be one, provided they are willing to put in consistent, disciplined, and focused efforts accompanied by deliberate practice of healthy writing habits.

Overcome Limiting Beliefs

- The perfectionist mindset is one major obstacle that often comes in the way of producing the first draft of our manuscript.

- Perfectionism is all about setting very high, impossible-to-achieve standards for oneself and others, always failing to meet them, and linking one's self-worth to the ability or inability to attain them.

- The healthy pursuit of excellence is helpful and energizing while the striving for artificial standards of perfection is unhealthy and disempowering.

- Perfectionism kills motivation and adds to further procrastination and blocking in writing.

- Some practical tips on overcoming perfectionism: have a down-to-earth attitude towards writing and don't think of it as your magnum opus; accept that we all mistakes; learn to make quick decisions on trivial issues; set your productivity goals realistically (even writing 5 minutes a day is a sign of progress than nothing); focus on the process of writing, not on the final goal or what comes after that; seek support.

- Know that your "inner critic" is ever-vigilant, always judging you and others around you for its aim is to not allow you to do anything productively and achieve your goals.

- Avoid negatively labeling yourself or others for it sends wrong signals to the brain and develops an unhealthy critical mentality that is counterproductive.

- Silence your inner critic by separating yourself from it by taking few deep breaths, jotting down its demand when you first notice it surfacing, take another deep breath and carry on with mindful writing.

Set SMART goals

- The concept of setting SMART goals takes a mammoth, vaguely-defined writing project and breaks it into Specific, Measurable, Attainable, Relevant and Time-bound goals.

- Specific goals help you to focus on narrow and concrete tasks that make up your writing product at the end.

- Your specific goal should have a measurable outcome as well as metrics that help you assess your progress towards the goal.

- Make your goal attainable by being realistic and identifying what is needed to get there.

- Everything you do should be relevant to your goal and not deviate you or get you sidetracked.

- Specific, measurable, attainable, and relevant goals that don't have deadlines are never completed.

- In setting writing and other goals, place your emphasis on efforts and reward your efforts rather than emphasizing the final outcome and punishing yourself for not achieving it.

Create Your Daily To-Do Lists

- Lack of planning in writing leads to stressful binge writing accompanied by unhealthy euphoric states and high error rates in writing.

- Take 20-30 minutes on a Friday or Sunday to plan for the week ahead.

- Based on your weekly plan, create your daily To-Do lists (including scheduling your writing

session) and stick them in your weekly
calendar.

- Remember there will always be too much to do
  and too little time to do them in. All you can do
  is to be selective, set clear priorities and focus on
  completing the most important tasks.

Write Daily

- The single most useful writing advice offered by
  almost all productive writers and writing
  coaches is this: write daily!

- When we make a conscious choice to write
  daily, we are forming a life-long healthy habit.

- Previous as well as contemporary research tells
  us that the most productive writers are those
  who write daily in small chunks of time.

- There are a number of benefits to writing in the
  morning for academicians. However, if your
  schedule doesn't permit it, choose a time that
  you can stick to every day.

- Employ the freewriting technique to get lots of
  messy first drafts and save editing for the future
  drafts.

- For most academicians, writing 30 minutes a day seems to be an achievable goal.

- Writing is thinking. Use writing to catalyze your critical thinking process.

Set a Timer When you Write

- Your focus and productivity is much higher when you have to get something done within a specific time interval than when you have all the time to get it done.

- Unless you have already established consistent and steady levels of daily writing output, it is a good idea to stop when the timer goes off. This builds a healthy and daily habit of writing.

- Give yourself a treat at the end of your writing session as it adds color to your writing routine and positively reinforces your writing habit.

- Track your daily writing progress by the amount of time you spent writing (or word count or number of pages) and review it at the end of the week to identify and reinforce habits that contribute to productive writing.

Eliminate Distractions

- Distractions can have external or internal origins, but how we choose to respond to those distractions always rests with us.

- A clean, well-lit, organized writing space helps you to remain calm and focused.

- It can be distracting to keep all sorts of programs open while you write, especially your e-mail program.

- The best way to eliminate online distractions is to simply unplug the Ethernet cable or to turn off the Wi-Fi before you start to write.

- When you are interrupted, take a moment to reflect on what should be your response based on the urgency of the interruption. If it is not that urgent, carry on with your writing and attend to it later.

- Rambling, disoriented thoughts that take away our focus are far more difficult to deal with than the external interruptions.

- Have a pen and paper next to you while you write and note down any nagging thoughts such as unfulfilled obligations, housekeeping activities, etc.

- Research has shown that daily practice of some sort of meditation can actually help improve our focus and concentration.

Be Accountable

- The nature of academic work has least built-in accountability when it comes to writing.

- Rewarding ourselves abundantly after completing our scheduled writing session is the best form of self-accountability.

- Contrary to the popular belief that shutting ourselves up in isolation and writing can improve productivity, research related to faculty development has shown that accountability and support can actually help achieve sustainable and steady levels of productivity.

- Connecting with a writing group or a small community of writers provides you with the opportunity to talk about your writing to others, mutually exchange ideas, and share the struggles you face with your writing.

- There are many free or fee-based online writing groups to facilitate accountability and mutual sharing of feedback and support.

A Note to the Reader

Thank you so much for reading this book!

I'd love to hear your feedback and thoughts on how you liked the book and how I can improve it further in the next edition.

Wishing you the very best,

Kasthurirangan "Rangan" Gopalakrishnan, Ph.D.

❧

Other Books by K. Gopalakrishnan

Climate Change, Energy, Sustainability and Pavements (Ed.)
Sustainable Bioenergy and Bioproducts (Ed.)
Nanotechnology in Civil Infrastructure (Ed.)
Sustainable Highways, Pavements and Materials
Soft Computing in Green and Renewable Energy Systems (Ed.)
Sustainable and Resilient Critical Infrastructure Systems (Ed.)
Intelligent and Soft Computing in Infrastructure Systems Engineering (Ed.)
Rutting in Flexible Airfield Pavements
Stripping Resistance of Asphalt Mixtures with Recycled Polymer Waste